JONAH AND THE WHALE

Contributing Writer
Marlene Targ Brill

Consultant
David M. Howard, Jr., Ph.D.

Illustrations
Gary Torrisi

Publications International, Ltd.

A long time ago, the people who lived in the city of Nineveh were making God very unhappy. They had forgotten about God and what He wanted them to do. So God spoke to Jonah, a man from Israel. God told Jonah to go to Nineveh and tell the people there that God was going to punish them for their wicked ways.

Jonah was afraid. He did not want to make the long trip to Nineveh. The people of Nineveh were enemies of the people of Israel.

Jonah decided to hide. He packed some food and money and started out for Joppa, a busy city far from Nineveh.

When he reached the bustling city, Jonah became afraid again. "God will find me here and punish me," he worried. "I must go farther away." He decided to take a ship across the sea to Tarshish. He thought that even God would not be able to find him there.

Jonah paid for his ticket and got on the ship. He went into the ship's cabin and fell asleep. A short time later, the ship left the harbor.

Once the ship was out to sea, the sky changed greatly. A large thunderstorm swept over the sea. The rolling waves threatened to break the ship apart. The frightened sailors threw the ship's cargo into the sea. They hoped that a lighter ship would make it through the storm.

The danger did not go away. Each man prayed to his own god, but the storm continued. The captain woke Jonah. "Get up," he ordered. "Call on your God. Perhaps He can save us."

The sailors thought that someone had brought the storm upon them. They cast lots (which was like drawing straws) to see who was causing all the problems. It soon became clear that Jonah was the one responsible for their troubles. Everyone on the ship had questions for him.

Jonah explained that he was running away from God. The men were even more afraid. "What will we do to quiet the sea?"

Jonah now realized that there was nowhere to hide from God. So he told the sailors to throw him into the sea. The sailors did not want to throw Jonah overboard. They tried everything to bring the ship back to land. But the winds were too strong. Finally, they lifted Jonah and threw him into the stormy sea.

At once the storm cleared. God sent a mighty fish to swallow Jonah. He lived in the belly of the fish for three days and three nights. During this time, Jonah prayed, thanking God for letting him live. God heard Jonah's prayers and commanded the fish to swim close to shore. There, it opened its mouth and tossed Jonah onto dry land.

Then God again ordered Jonah to go to Nineveh. This time, Jonah obeyed.

Jonah traveled to Nineveh. "In forty days God will destroy Nineveh," he cried to all the people there.

God's words reached the king of Nineveh. He rose from his throne, took off his royal robes, and put on rough rags. Then the king sat in ashes. He ruled that every person and animal should go without food and water. They were to stop behaving in their evil ways. They were to pray to God to forgive them so Nineveh could be saved.

God heard the people's prayers and forgave them. He saved their city. The people rejoiced. Only Jonah was unhappy. Why had God made him travel all this way only to change His mind?

Jonah left the city. After a while, he sat down and looked toward the city's east wall.

God caused a vine to grow over Jonah. The plant shaded Jonah from the burning sun. Jonah was very happy about the vine.

The next morning, God sent a worm to attack the vine. Jonah awoke to find his beloved plant withered. He was angry.

"Is it right for you to be angry about the vine?" God asked Jonah. "You loved this vine that you did not grow. It was only on earth one day," said God. "But you want me to destroy Nineveh. I cared for this city over many years."

This is how God showed Jonah that He loves and forgives all people who turn to Him.